Seafood Salad

Published by KENTON PUBLISHING
The Granary
Hatham Green Lane
Stansted
SEVENOAKS
Kent TN15 7PL
www.kentonpublishing.co.uk

First published in Great Britain in 2008 by KENTON PUBLISHING
ISBN 978-0-9546223-3-6
2 4 6 8 10 9 7 5 3 1

Designed by Brigitte Bell Design

Production by Bookplan Production Services

Printed in the UK by Cambridge University Press

Seafood Salad

SEAFOOD RECIPES *from the world-renowned*
PRIDE OF BRITAIN HOTELS

In support of the RNLI

CONTENTS

RECIPES

POEMS

PRIDE OF BRITAIN HOTELS

Foreword
By Paul Milsom

In the 1960s as the owner of Maison Talbooth, my father, Gerald Milsom, was one of the pioneers of the country house movement and a great champion of the independent hotelier.

However, he quickly realised that if he was to get his marketing message across to a new breed of travel-hungry consumers he would have to join a consortium. It was for this reason that in 1964 he became only the second UK member of Relais & Chateaux.

They were great days for those, like Gerald, who were driven on to raise the standards of their hotels from the mediocrity that prevailed at the time. The result was the creation of some of the finest hotels this country has to offer.

However, by 1979, Gerald had come to blows with the French management of Relais & Chateaux. He felt the members did not have enough say in the way in which the expanding consortium was run. In fact, he was thrown out of the organisation just a few days after speaking out.

This was a severe and unplanned setback as he felt his business would suffer if he didn't find a replacement. So, Gerald did what all good entrepreneurs do when confronted with this sort of predicament, he set up his own consortium.

This consortium, though, would be different. It would be all British and, crucially, it would be run by its members, for its members.

So, in 1982 Pride of Britain Hotels was born with an eager band of 12 founder members. Fortunately the 80s saw a great growth in the number of quality country house hotels, with the result that the original 12 quickly swelled and the current membership is now approaching 40 of the finest privately owned hotels in Britain.

In 2007, we celebrated 25 years of POB – as the organisation is affectionately known. Hotels and hoteliers have come and gone during those years but all would agree it has been a marvellous organisation to be part of and above all it's been a lot of fun.

In this book we have included recipes for the finest seafood dishes from chefs at some of our member hotels around the UK. Each recipe is accompanied by a poem and details of the heroism of the lifeboat crews at RNLI stations near to our hotels.

I hope Seafood Salad will raise funds for the RNLI, will inspire some of you to visit our wonderful hotels and tempt you to cook for yourself the most fantastic food our seas have to offer.

Gerald Milsom OBE, founder of Pride of Britain Hotels

Seafood Salad

There are whelks and winkles
Ling and lobster
Turbot, plaice and oysters,
There are even whales
And slow sea snails
Around the monkfish cloisters.

You'll find crabs and dabs
And brill and bream
And mussels in our ballad
A dogfish, garfish
Codfish, starfish
Tossed in our seafood salad.

J.D.

HEROES OF THE SEA
A brief history of the RNLI

More than a thousand people each year owe their lives to the calm courage of Britain's lifeboat crews.

For over 150 years RNLI volunteers have risked their lives putting to sea in all weathers to rescue the crews of boats in distress.

The idea of an organised national institution for rescue at sea was the brainchild of one man, Lt Col Sir William Hillary.

This extraordinary former soldier settled on the Isle of Man, forming and leading the island's first-ever volunteer lifeboat crew – despite not being able to swim. In that time he helped save an astonishing 305 lives.

During his time leading the lifeboat crew in the island's capital, Douglas, he campaigned for a national lifeboat organisation.

One of his pamphlets on the subject came to the attention of Thomas Wilson, MP for the City of London.

It was largely through Wilson's efforts that a meeting was held at the City of London Tavern on 4th March 1824 and the outcome was Britain's first coordinated sea rescue service.

Given the rather cumbersome title of the National Institution for the Preservation of Life from Shipwreck, it became known rather unfortunately as the Shipwreck Institution.

Thirty years later its name was changed to the Royal National Lifeboat Institution.

On his tombstone Lt Col Sir William Hillary, Bt, is credited as the founder of the RNLI and to this day, the Douglas lifeboat is named after him.

*In Danger's Hour – A History of the RNLI by Patrick Howarth is published by Hamlyn.

Train one, save many

A Brotherhood of Lifeboat Men

Cornish, Scottish, Welsh and others,
A truly close-knit band of brothers.
Joining forces on the quay,
For those in peril on the sea.

Welsh and Irish join together,
Setting out what'ere the weather,
When comes the call at work or quay
From those in peril on the sea.

Irish, Scottish and the rest,
Sail from north and east and west,
When comes the call at home or quay,
From those in peril on the sea.

Scottish, Cornish, all set forth,
Sailing east and south and north,
When comes the call at rest or quay,
From those in peril on the sea.

Celtic, English and the others,
The lifeboat men are truly brothers.
Joining forces on the quay,
For those in peril on the sea.

Ode to the John Dory

The John Dory is the finest fish,
That ever graced a plate or dish.
A fish with flesh so fine and sweet,
It makes you want to eat and eat.
John Dory, also called St. Peter,
Touched by god, so none taste sweeter.
Pan fried, poached or from the grill,
With lemon butter, fresh chopped dill.

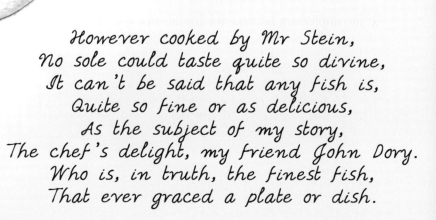

However cooked by Mr Stein,
No sole could taste quite so divine,
It can't be said that any fish is,
Quite so fine or as delicious,
As the subject of my story,
The chef's delight, my friend John Dory.
Who is, in truth, the finest fish,
That ever graced a plate or dish.

JOHN DORY & LOBSTER SAUSAGE
with Lobster & Caviar Vinaigrette

This recipe is rather a long-winded affair but persevere because the end product is superb. And as lobsters are so expensive these days it makes sense to get as many portions as possible out of one fish. If you can, it is best to make the stock the day before and reduce it to a thick, syrupy sauce.

I always have plenty of crab and lobster bones in the freezer so that may be a problem for you. Ask your local fishmonger if he has any left over from when he cooks his shellfish, if not then you will have to remove the flesh first, then make the stock afterwards.

Larger lobsters are generally cheaper because nobody wants tough, big fish - they are even cheaper if you can buy them straight from the fishermen themselves.

FOR THE MOUSSE
1 LIVE 4 LB LOBSTER
2 JOHN DORY FILLETS
2 EGG WHITES
SALT, PEPPER
APPROX 3/4 (355 ML) OF A PINT WHIPPING CREAM

FOR THE SALAD
4 OZ (115G) COUSCOUS
1 SMALL RED PEPPER, DICED
1/4 PINT (120 ML) FISH STOCK
DASH OLIVE OIL
SALT, PEPPER
1 SMALL HEAD LOLLO ROSSO

FOR THE STOCK
LOBSTER BONES
1 SMALL ONION
2 CARROTS
1 STICK OF CELERY
1 SMALL LEEK
1 BULB OF FENNEL
SMALL BULB OF GARLIC
1 TABLESPOON OF TOMATO PASTE
A LITTLE PARSLEY, THYME AND BASIL
1/2 LEMON
1/4 PINT (120 ML) DRY, WHITE WINE
WATER

Place a pan on the stove, fill with cold water and bring to the boil. Add a little salt and a dash of white wine vinegar.

Next the unpleasant bit, take the live lobster and with a sharp knife, cut through the head and halfway up the body in one movement straight through to the board, this will kill the lobster instantly. Some chefs place them straight into the boiling water, okay this will kill them.... eventually, but the R.S.P.C.A. tell us that a live lobster can actually live in boiling water for up to eleven seconds. I think the poor creature is in a real state already, so I believe that it is best done the more humane way.

Plunge the lobster into the rapidly boiling water for approximately ten seconds, then straight into iced water. This arrests the cooking straight away (the reason for this is to make the flesh shrink away from the shell, so it can be removed easily).

Remove all the flesh from the tail and take out the black alimentary canal, chill well. Put the claws back into the simmering water and cook for a further ten minutes. Cool under running cold water, drain and chill (this is used for the garnish).

Put the lobster flesh, egg whites, salt, and the John Dory fillets into a Magimix and blend on a slow speed to start with. Once the mixture is roughly chopped then turn up the speed and puree until the mixture is as smooth as possible. This should take approximately three to four minutes but no longer as the flesh will warm up due to the friction of the blades, if this happens remove the bowl and chill for a few minutes.

Once chilled, and using a rubber ended spatula, place all the contents into a medium stainless steel bowl. Using a small plastic scraper pass the flesh through a fine sieve, this takes out all the unwanted sinews and bones, a job which takes a few minutes. Luckily, I have apprentices to do this painstaking task.

Chill again, then gradually beat in the cream making sure that you do not add too much at a time, the mixture should stay thick. After you have beaten in approximately $3/4$ of the cream you then have to test it. Take a little of the mixture in a warm teaspoon and place it into a small pan of simmering water,

BINDON COUNTRY HOUSE

Mike Davies

Our Head Chef Mike Davies spent 3 years as Head Chef at Holne Chase, Devon which held 2AA rosettes for the quality of its cuisine, before moving back to Somerset to join us at Bindon House.

Following up a schoolboy ambition to be a chef, he started training at the age of 16 at The Castle, Taunton. He worked along side former Head Chef of the Year Phil Vickery for seven years & then successor Richard Guest for 2 years. Michael played an instrumental part in their achieving a Michelin Star & 4 AA Rosettes.

"I enjoy cooking locally sourced, traditional English Cuisine & am delighted to be working back in Somerset again. I like to produce menus that are focused on the seasons, as they are more flexible & means I can take advantage of the best ingredients available on any one day so our Table d'Hote menu changes daily in addition to the A La Carte menu which changes seasonally."

let it poach for a few seconds until it is completely cooked through. Remove it from the saucepan with a slotted spoon and gently squeeze the cooked mousse, it should just give a slight resistance. If the mousse is too firm then add a little more cream but be careful, too much cream will result in the finished sausages collapsing once cooked.

When you are happy with the mousse, check the seasoning, cover with cling film, and chill again. Take the claws from the refrigerator and place on a chopping board. With a sharp, heavy knife, crack the claws and remove all the flesh, take out any shell from the inside and chop into small cubes. Add the meat to the finished mousse.

To make the sausages you will need a large piping bag (no tube is necessary) a spoon and a box of cling film. Fill the bag in the usual way and pipe onto the cling film the size that you prefer, cut the film and roll up one end of the sausage taking special care not to roll the cling film into the mousse. Secure the end with a little string, repeat the procedure with the other end, chill well.

Bring to the boil a small pan of water and turn down so that it barely simmers. Pop in the sausages and gently poach for approximately eight minutes, remove with a slotted spoon and place in iced water to arrest the cooking.

In a large saucepan place the lobster bones, vegetables and a little olive oil. Cook over a moderate heat until they both take a little colour then add the water and wine. Bring to the boil and skim off any scum. Simmer for a couple of minutes then add the herbs, lemon, and tomato paste and cook for a further forty minutes. When cooked, strain in a colander and reduce the liquor in a clean saucepan until you end up with a thick, syrupy sauce. Then strain through a fine sieve to remove any tiny particles of shell.

FOR THE DRESSING
2 TABLESPOONS BALSAM VINEGAR
1 DESSERTSPOON DIJON MUSTARD
4 TABLESPOONS OF OLIVE OIL
THE REDUCED STOCK (SEE PREVIOUS RECIPE)
SALT AND PEPPER
LEMON JUICE

THE GARNISH
CHOPPED, DESEEDED TOMATO
CHOPPED CHIVES
CAVIAR (IF YOU ARE FEELING RICH)

Place the lobster stock in a liquidizer along with the rest of the ingredients apart from the oil. Liquidize and, when thoroughly incorporated, gradually add the oil. The mixture will emulsify like a runny mayonnaise then remove and check the seasoning. Add the garnish and reserve.
Boil the fish stock and pour over the couscous. Cover and cool, add the salt and pepper, diced pepper, and adjust the seasoning, arrange in the middle of the plate with the picked, washed, Lollo rosso.

Warm the sausages in a small pan of simmering water for approximately three minutes. Remove and cut open with a sharp knife, be careful not to slice into the sausage, place on top of the couscous and lettuces and spoon over the dressing, serve immediately.

GRILLED JOHN DORY
with Lime
and Ginger Butter Sauce

4 x 6OZ JOHN DORY FILLETS

LIGHT SOY SAUCE

JUICE OF 3 LIMES

6 OZ SOFTENED BUTTER

GRAPE SEED OIL

HALF A TABLESPOON OF FINELY CHOPPED ROOT GINGER

SMALL BUNCH OF FRESH CORIANDER

SERVES 4

Make a marinade by combining the juice of 1 lime, 2 tablespoons of light soy sauce, half the coriander and half of the chopped root ginger. Marinate the John Dory for 20 minutes. Dry the fillets on some kitchen paper, brush with oil and place under a very hot grill for 2 minutes on each side until just cooked. Remove to a warm plate and serve with 2 tablespoons full of lime and ginger butter sauce, garnish with picked coriander.

Lime and Ginger Butter Sauce
In a small pan combine the juice of 2 limes and half of the chopped root ginger. Bring to the boil and reduce by nine tenths, remove from the heat and gradually whisk in the softened butter, finish with chopped coriander, ground white pepper and soy sauce to taste. Serve immediately.

Poole Lifeboat Station

When the RNLI lifeboat was built at Sandbanks in Poole Harbour, Dorset, in 1865 the crew had to be taken to the station by coach from the Antelope Hotel in the High Street.

In 1906 Thanks of the Institution Inscribed on Vellum were awarded to Coxswain Richard Wills and Crew Members Thomas Wills, John Wills, Richard Cartridge, and Henry Russell for rescuing two men from a capsized fishing vessel.

The motor lifeboat, Thomas Kirk Wright arrived at the station in 1939 and the following year she was one of 19 lifeboats that took part in the evacuation of British Forces from Dunkirk.

In 1986 Thanks of the Institution Inscribed on Vellum were awarded to Crew Members David Coles, Steven Vince and Raymond Collin for rescuing two children from marshland.

And in 1995 Framed Letters of Thanks were presented to Coxswain Steve Vince and Crew Members Robert Doak and Geoffrey Langley for rescuing the yacht, Bloodhound.

And 2001 saw Framed Letters of Thanks awarded to Helmsman Gavin McGuinness and Crew Members Anne Millman and Paul Savage for rescuing four dinghies caught by a strong ebb tide and pinned against the chain ferry.

Station Honours
6 Framed Letters of Thanks
8 Thanks of the Institution Inscribed on Vellum
7 Silver Medals
1 Gold Medal

Brotherhood of Eels

Conger, Moray, Electric, and the others.
A wriggly, squiggly band of brothers.

Moray, Conger, Electric, and the rest,
Brothers to each other, to fishermen a pest.

Electric, Moray, Conger, and their kind,
Never have a cross word, so close are they affined.

Moray, Electric, Conger, and their kin,
Hold so close together, they only ever win.

Conger, Electric, Moray, and their breed,
Ever undivided, always will succeed.

Electric, Conger, Moray, and the others.
It's been said once before, the ocean's Band of Brothers

The Eclectic Eel

The eclectic eel haunts the decks
Of ancient wrecks
And collects the plunder,
That's gathered under
        the waves.

The eclectic eel steals
The things he feels,
Will decorate his lair,
To make it a fair
        cave.

The eclectic eel at first inspects,
And then collects
Each item of bounty,
That he considers his duty
        to save.

The eclectic eel will linger
Over precisely which finger
He should be taking,
From long drowned ratings'
        watery graves.

CURRIED CONWY
❦ QUAY MUSSELS ❧

1KG CONWY MUSSELS (OR ANY GOOD FRESH MUSSELS)
1 LARGE SHALLOT (FINELY DICED)
1 CLOVE OF GARLIC (CRUSHED)
RED CHILLI (FINE JULIENNE)
1 SPRING ONION (FINE JULIENNE)
4 SPRIGS OF CORIANDER
200 ML WHITE WINE
250 ML CREAM
20 G CURRY SPICE
1 TABLE SPOON OIL

Rinse mussels and remove barnacles and beards.
In a thick bottomed pan quickly fry shallot and garlic. Add mussels and curry spice then stir quickly, add white wine and cover for 2 minutes. Remove lid, add cream and boil for a further 2-3 minutes. Add some chopped coriander and serve mussels into bowls. Pour over cream sauce and garnish with picked coriander leaves, chilli and spring onion shreds.

BODYSGALLEN HALL

Gareth Jones
Having been with the Michelin starred Chester Grosvenor Hotel for seven years, Gareth has recently taken up the position of Head Chef at Bodysgallen Hall. His imaginative style and classic techniques, combined with his modern British cooking with a few light continental touches, convinces the hotel he will maintain and build on their three double AA Rosette cooking standard.

❦ MUSSEL, LEEK, ❧
SAFFRON & THYME SOUP

850 G / 2 LB FRESH MUSSELS

225 G / 8 OZ MIXED, ROUGHLY CUT, WHITE OF LEEK, WHITE ONION, CELERY

SMALL BUNCH OF LEMON THYME

225 ML / 8 FL OZ DRY VERMOUTH

50 G / 2 OZ EACH FINELY DICED, FENNEL, LEEK, CARROT

80 G / 3 OZ UNSALTED BUTTER

1 LITRE / 1 3/4 PINTS CHICKEN STOCK

PINCH OF SAFFRON

225 ML / 8 FL OZ DOUBLE CREAM

2 EGG YOLKS

4 TOMATOES, BLANCHED, PEELED, DESEEDED, DICED.

Carefully wash the mussels, discarding any that are open or damaged. Put the mussels, roughly cut white vegetables, thyme and vermouth in a large pan with a lid. Bring rapidly to the boil and cook for three to four minutes, stir once or twice and remove from the heat when all the mussels are open. Drain through a colander into a bowl; throw away any mussels that have not opened. Remove the mussels from their shells discarding their beards; keep them covered on a warm plate. Pass the mussel stock through a fine cloth to remove any sand.

Melt the butter, sweat the diced vegetables in the butter, add the mussel stock, the chicken stock and the saffron, bring to the boil and simmer until the vegetables are tender.

Mix the egg yolks and cream together in a bowl, stir in one ladle full of the hot stock, pour this mixture back into the soup and continue to heat but do not allow to boil. Add the warm mussels, some picked leaves of lemon thyme, and the diced tomato. Season with cayenne pepper and salt to taste.

Conwy Lifeboat Station

In June 1966 an inshore lifeboat station was established at Conwy, north Wales with a D class inshore lifeboat.

Just four years later Thanks of the Institution Inscribed on Vellum were awarded to crew members Brian Jones, Ronald Craven and Trevor Jones for rescuing two men from the cabin cruiser, Fulmar, which had broken down west of Llandudno.

In winds gusting up to force seven and in shallow water with heavy broken seas, the inshore lifeboat had to make two runs alongside so the two men could jump to safety from the stricken Fulmar.

On June 21, 1995 the D class lifeboat, D-482 Arthur Bate was placed on service. This was provided from the bequest of the late Arthur Charles Bate.

Nine years later the D class lifeboat, D-627 Arthur Bate 11 was placed on service at Conwy.

In March 2008 the lifeboat was called to rescue 12 sheep marooned by the high spring tide, which had overflowed into their field.

Two of the volunteer crew members waded through shoulder-deep water and herded the sheep to safety. One, unfortunately, was found to be dead and another barely alive.

Station Honours
3 Thanks of the Institution Inscribed on Vellum

A Cod's Lament

GIVE MY CONDIMENTS TO THE CHEF!
(We who are about to fry, salute you)

It's never a pleasure being eaten,
There's no fun in becoming a snack,
I've more than a hunch,
That it hurts to be lunch,
(Courage is not what I lack)!
First course? Or main? Ain't amusing,
Take a moment, and give me a thought.
Just where is the thrill
Being under a grill?
Browned off, and totally fraught!
I really don't want to get seasoned,
Put away both the pepper and salt,
Lose the lemon and oil,
Forget the tin foil,
Being tasty! It isn't my fault.

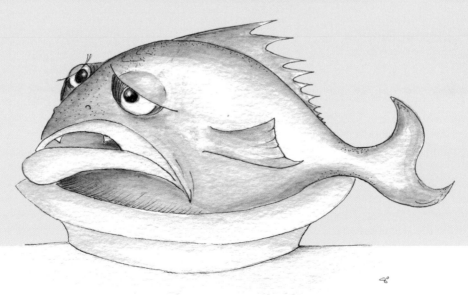

❧ CORNISH FISH PIE ❧
with Cockles & Mussels

1LB OF EACH FISH DICED SALMON, COD, HADDOCK AND
POLLACK/WHITING
8 OZ (230 G) MUSSELS
8OZ (230 G) COCKLES & CLAMS
3 PINTS (1.4 L) FISH STOCK
WHITE WINE
FLAT PARSLEY, TARRAGON, CELERY LEAVES
ONION, CARROT, LEEK, FENNEL AND CELERY
(DICED IN 3-4MM PIECES)
4 OZ (115 G) BUTTER/ 4 OZ FLOUR
4 OZ (115 G) PRAWNS

POTATO TOPPING
6 LB (2.75 KG) OF POTATO CUT INTO 1.5CM CUBES
2 PINTS MILK
NUTMEG, GARLIC, BLACK PEPPER AND SEA SALT
BREADCRUMBS
MELTED BUTTER

MAKES 15 SERVINGS

Preparation

To make topping - put the potato dice into a tray with milk and seasonings, and bake until cooked and almost all the milk has been absorbed - remove and cool down.

Make a roux (blond) with the butter and flour, then make into a fish veloute with the fish stock. Add cream to make a velvety fish sauce.

Sweat down the diced vegetables in butter until soft. Add the diced fish, a little white wine and fish stock, and lightly steam.

Separately steam open the mussels/clams and cockles in white wine, and pick out the meat from the shells.

Save the liquor from the shellfish and add to the fish veloute.

Now add the fish veloute to the lightly steamed fish mixture and delicately bind together. Finally add the chopped fresh herbs.

Chill immediately.

To serve - fill an oval fish pie dish with the chilled mixture.

Then put on a topping of the diced potato, sprinkle with the breadcrumbs and drizzle with melted butter - bake until hot and golden brown - serve with a wedge of lemon and a sprig of flat parsley.

CALCOT MANOR

Michael Croft
Michael Croft started his career under Michel Bourdin of the Connaught Hotel, London. He moved on to the Gravetye Manor in East Grinstead, followed by a year as an Egon Ronay Inspector of Hotels and Restaurants. He became senior Sous Chef at the Ritz Hotel, London and Head Chef responsible for the re-opening of the Mirabelle Restaurant in London.
He is currently director and Executive Head Chef of Calcot Manor Hotel, Tetbury.

CRAYFISH SOUP
under a Puff Pastry Dome

24 SMALL CRAYFISH

2 OZ / 55 G BUTTER

2 OZ / 55 G EACH OF; CARROT, ONION, CELERY, AND LEEKS, WASHED PEELED AND DICED

1 SPRIG OF THYME

1 BAY LEAF

SMALL BUNCH OF PARSLEY

2 FL OZ / 60 ML BRANDY

5 FL OZ / 150 ML DRY WHITE WINE

1 TABLESPOON TOMATO PUREE

1 OZ / 30 G PLAIN FLOUR

1 PT / 475 ML FISH STOCK

2 FL OZ / 60 ML WHIPPING CREAM

12 OZ / 430 G PUFF PASTRY

1 EGG AND MILK FOR EGG WASH

4 DEEP, OVENPROOF LIONS HEAD SOUP BOWLS

Cook the crayfish in boiling water for 3 minutes, refresh and shell them reserving the tails. Crush the shells. Cook the vegetables, thyme, bay leaf, parsley and the crayfish shells in the butter until the vegetables begin to brown. Season with a little salt and freshly milled white pepper. Add the brandy and ignite, when the flame dies down add the white wine, bring to the boil, and allow to simmer for 5 minutes. Add the tomato puree and flour. Whisk until the flour is properly incorporated, add the fish stock and bring back to the boil, turn down and allow to simmer for 15 minutes.
Pass through a very fine sieve or a muslin cloth. Return the soup to a clean saucepan, add the cream bring back to the boil, correct the seasoning, allow to cool.

Put 6 crayfish tails into each of the soup bowls pour in the cooled soup. Roll out the puff pastry to a thickness of $1/8$ of an inch. Cut out 4 rings of pastry 1 inch wider than the soup bowls. Egg wash a 1 inch ring around the outside of the soup bowl and cover with the puff pastry so that it is like a drum skin, crimp the edges, egg wash the pastry and bake in a pre-heated oven, 180 degrees for 25 minutes.

Douglas Lifeboat Station

The first lifeboat was built at Douglas, Isle of Man in 1802, funded by the Duke of Atholl and built by Henry Greathead who built the first-ever lifeboat in 1789.

In 1881 Douglas's Number 2 lifeboat capsized after rescuing 16 people from the barge, Lebu. Tragically four lifeboat crew members and seven of the rescued seamen drowned.

Ten years later, Shore Helper W Gordon died after he was injured while helping to launch the lifeboat.

In 1924 the station's first motor lifeboat was placed on service and kept in a new boathouse.

And in1997 A Vellum was presented to the station to commemorate the 150th anniversary of the death of Sir William Hillary.

Two years later Coxswain Robert Corran was awarded an MBE in the Queen's Birthday Honours.

In 2002 the RSPCA awarded a commendation for rescuing a heifer stranded on a rocky outcrop. The heifer jumped into the sea, where it was lassoed and gently towed to Port Soderick beach.

Station Honours
1 Thanks of the Institution Inscribed on Vellum
15 Silver Medals
5 Gold Medals

Weather or not

Below the waves,
It never snows on mountain tops,
No sound of gently falling rain drops,

(wind and drizzle, sleet and mizzle,
do not disturb the deep).

Beneath the sea,
Fog never ever forms or lingers
No touch felt of Jack Frost's chilly fingers,

(wind and drizzle, sleet and mizzle
never stir our sleep).

Underneath the ocean,
We find no need nor wish
To hear good news from Michael fish,

(wind and drizzle, sleet and mizzle
cannot make us weep).

Sir Penfold Plaice

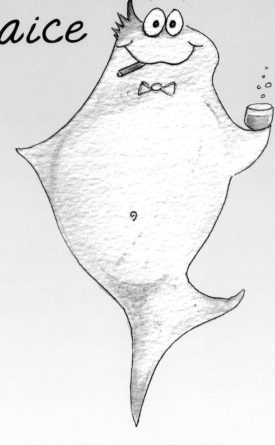

Sir Penfold was a gourmand
And committed bon viveur,
A philanthropic gentleman,
And beguiling raconteur.

He liked to wine and dine - and did,
To such a great degree,
That the inches on the measuring tape,
Crept up to forty three.

He crashed into his bed one night,
His wife shot to the ceiling,
And when she landed on the floor,
She lost all sense and feeling.

Sir Penfold found her still and prone,
Upon the floor next day,
His conscience smote him deeply,
And he viewed her with dismay.

Her Ladyship was not amused,
When consciousness returned,
And Sir Penfold's kindly gestures,
Were very roundly spurned.

A lifestyle change was put in place,
No fat, no wine, no gin,
Just salad, rice and vegetables.
And work-outs at the gym.

A bicycle and pedal power,
Replaced the chauffeured car,
With strict instructions,
"there and back,
No stopping at the bar!"

At six weeks on the new regime,
With not a drop of wine,
The inches on the measuring tape,
Dropped down to 29.

Though Sir Penfold's still a gourmand,
And committed bon viveur,
A philanthropic gentleman,
And beguiling raconteur.

He's happy being fit and lean
So nowadays he tends
To frugality on weekdays
And indulgence at weekends.

❧ GRILLED PLAICE ❧
with Green Sauce, Shrimps & Lime

4 WHOLE PLAICE, HEADS OFF, CLEANED AND SKINNED

200 G BROWN SHRIMPS

450 G MAYONNAISE

1 BUNCH OF WATERCRESS

50 G EACH OF SPINACH, BASIL, DILL & PARSLEY

FRESH LIME

BUTTER

OLIVE OIL

Season plaice with salt and pepper and paint with butter and olive oil.
Chop herbs, spinach and watercress, leaving some for garnish, then stir into mayonnaise.
Add shrimps, season and finish with lime juice. Grill plaice on both sides till golden.
Serve with a generous dollop of green sauce, lime and buttered Jersey Royal potatoes.

THE CHESTER GROVESNOR

Jones in London.

Simon Radley

Executive Chef Simon Radley, started at The Chester Grosvernor and Spa in 1986, when he joined the hotel as a Chef de Partie and went on to become Head Chef in the space of seven years.

During the hotel's closure for extensive refurbishment in 1987, Simon took a 12-month secondment to broaden his experience, working under Chef Paul Gayler at Inigo

In 1991, his skills were further enhanced when, acting as The Chester Grosvenor's ambassador, he spent time in the legendary Penninsula Hotel in Hong Kong and The Oriental in Bangkok,

consistently rated by the international business community as one of the best hotels in the world.

In order to widen his experience, Simon moved to New Hall, near Birmingham, in 1994 as Executive Chef and then took over the same role at Nunsmere Hall at Oakmere, Cheshire.

Simon returned to the Chester Grosvenor and Spa in June 1998 and has established his mark on the hotel with the retention of a Michelin star for the 16th consecutive year.

❧ TUNA TARTARE ❧

16 OZ / 450 G FRESH TUNA FILLET
2 OZ / 55 G SEA SALT
1/2 OZ / 15 G CASTER SUGAR
1/2 TEASPOON OF SALTPETRE
JUICE OF I LIME
I TABLESPOON SOY SAUCE
I TEASPOON FINELY SHREDDED PICKLED GINGER
MIXED WASHED LEAVES
SMALL BUNCH OF CHERVIL
6 FL OZ / 175 ML CRÈME FRAICHE
2 TEASPOONS WASABI SAUCE

Dry the tuna on kitchen paper, combine the sugar, salt and saltpetre, sprinkle evenly over the tuna, cover and refrigerate for 3 hours. Wash off the mixture, dry with kitchen paper and chill for at least 5 hours. Cut the tuna into small cubes add the limejuice and soy sauce mix together. Mix the crème fraiche and wasabi sauce.
Arrange the mixed leaves on a chilled plate, using a round cutter form the tuna into a scone shape and place in the middle. Using two teaspoons form an egg shape out of the sauce and put on top of the tartare, garnish with a pinch of shredded pickled ginger and picked chervil.

A salt water croc with a grin,
Said, "I know that you think it a sin,
But to eat folk is fine,
With a nice glass of wine,
If that person just chanced to fall in."

Fleetwood Lifeboat Station

The first lifeboat station at Fleetwood, Lancs, was built in 1859 and within a year, Captain Edward Wasey RN had been awarded three Silver Medals for helping rescue a total of 21 people from the sea. In 1949 a Bronze medal was awarded to Coxswain James Leadbetter for rescuing eight crew from the ketch, Alpha. Six of the crew were rescued a second time after they returned to the vessel, in spite of warnings.

An inshore lifeboat (ILB) station was established in 1966 with a D class lifeboat. This was kept in a small house and launched across the beach.

In 1984 the Thanks of the Institution Inscribed on Vellum was awarded to Second Coxswain Stephen James Musgrave for rescuing a windsurfer three and a half miles off Fleetwood.

And in 1985 the Ralph Glister Award for the most meritorious service carried out in 1984 was awarded to Helmsman Stephen Musgrave and Crew Members Barrie Farmer and David Owen for the windsurfer rescue.

Station Honours
2 Thanks of the Institution Inscribed on Vellum
12 Silver Medals
1 Bronze Medal

Profishional Jealousy

There's a whiting who lives in the channel,
Thinks he's the best bard of all time.
He spends all his days
In poetical haze,
Writing verses that never quite rhyme.

He does "favours" by giving recitals,
In the mussel beds down in the deep,
But the only reaction,
To this benefaction
Is to send them all straight off to sleep.

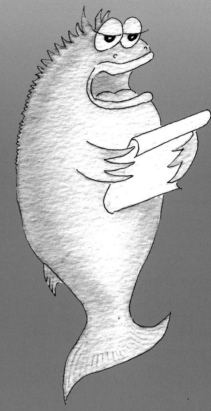

He's convinced that one day he'll be famous,
Like Wordsworth or Shelley or Frost,
But the polite fishes say,
"Will you please go away!!"
While the rest of us just say, "get lost!"

This whiting's a fool and a dreamer,
Why, it's as plain as the nose on your face,
That the bard of the sea,
Isn't him, but it's ME,
I'm Percy the Poetical Plaice.